Foster Parenting

A Basic Guide to Creating a Loving, Comforting and Stable Home

by Linda Siegmund

Published in Canana by:

Linda Siegmund

© Copyright 2014 – Linda Siegmund

ISBN-13: 978-1505323986
ISBN-10: 1505323983

Table of Contents

Preface

Thank you.

I'm thanking you not just because you've decided to buy this book, but because by buying it I know you're thinking about becoming a Foster parent. I'd go into the statistics of children who are left homeless each year due to neglect or mistreatment, but I know you already know them. So thank you for taking this step not only to become a foster parent but to become a **good** foster parent.

My husband and I have had eight foster kids living with us for the lifetime of our marriage. With each successive child who has blessed us with their presence we've learned a lot that has made living with the next child a much easier and more rewarding experience. But I wish that we had known a lot of this stuff when we started off with our first child. I wish I had some sort of guide to help me deal with the daily challenges that came with having a new little friend. It is why I decided to write this book.

This book will answer questions such as;

- How can I prepare myself and my family for a new addition?
- What can I expect on the first few days after receiving my foster child?
- How can I ease their transition from living with their family to living with my family?
- What should I do in case of behavioral and

emotional problems with my child?

- How can I encourage my child to take an interest in school?
- How do I deal with hostile parents or relatives?
- How can I make sure that I do not get overwhelmed emotionally or physically?
- When it is time to let go, how will I make it easier for me, my family and my foster child?

And many, many more questions.

Thanks again for buying this book, I hope you enjoy it!

Chapter 1:
Easing Your Child's Entrance

Do you remember your first day of school?

If you don't, close your eyes and imagine yourself as a six year old.

You woke up that morning with a knot at the pit of your stomach. It was finally THAT day; the day you were going to be separated from Mommy for the WHOLE day. At breakfast you felt a rush of nausea when Mommy asked you if you were ready for school. You nodded but a small tear still slipped out. There she was to tell you that it would be okay. The teachers were really nice at your new school and you would make new friends and in about six hours you were going to see each other anyway. Her words calmed you down enough to get you out of the house.

At school you held on to Mommy or Daddy's hand

tightly as they introduced you to your new teacher. She didn't dress like Mommy, she didn't talk like Mommy… in fact everything about her was so different that you weren't sure you were going to like her or that she was going to like you. You looked around the class to find strange small faces staring back at you and wondered which of them would be your first friend or if they would even agree to be your friend. However like the brave champ you are, you waved a sad goodbye to Mommy and prepared to start school.

Does this experience sound familiar? It's kind of the same experience your foster child gets when they are coming to you for the first time. Only it's not the same.

I know you want me to tell you that everything you have done so far, from the extensive training classes, the rigorous efforts to get your license, will be rewarded in the form of a well behaved miniature adult who you will love on first sight and who will be just as excited to have you for a foster parent. I know you hope your first day is going to roses and sunshine. It might be.

In all probability it won't.

The home your child is coming from has been broken by strife, abuse and/or neglect. Your child has no one s/he trusts to tell them that it is going to be just fine and the place they are going isn't going to be so bad. In fact grown ups have probably been such a disappointment to them so far that they do not trust any reassurances they give.

You are not the kindly teacher who will be helping them learn about the world around them. You are the woman or man trying to usurp their parents' role in their life. The happy children in your home remind them of the friends they have lost by being yanked so abruptly from their own home. If your children are biological, the feelings of isolation are even more intense because they feel like they do not belong and are encroaching on someone else's property. They don't even have the option of going back home in the evening when 'school' is over. In fact they don't know when and/or **if** they'll be going back home.

Prepare For The Worst

Now that you know, what this child visiting you is thinking, perhaps you can better understand why in all likelihood, you won't be getting an angel. Hope for it, but to do not expect it. Preparing for the worst means you will be less likely to be disappointed when you get your first foster child and they are not perfect. And don't think they won't tune in to your disappointment. Children are more intuitive than we give them credit for, especially children who have been forced to grow up before their time.

So what is the absolute worst you can get?

For every foster parent 'worst' is a relative thing. We experience and perceive situations differently. Write down a list of the things that you think would most annoy you about having little house guests. Items in your list may include stealing, disrespectful to authority, refusal to participate in school, defecating everywhere but the bathroom, atheist (if you're religious), lack of table manners, keeps running away etc. Be as specific as possible in your list.

Now, some of the items on your list may feel petty as you write them down. However, nothing is too minor to put on this list. The better you know the things that irritate you, the more a handle you will have on your emotions and reaction when they do occur and it's not like you're going to share it with anyone anyway. Think of it as an exercise in self-exploration.

For every item on your list, write down how you will react to the problem. How will you deal with it? The way you choose should be appropriate to the situation, calm, respectful to the child and sensitive to their background. If for interest you do not like it when someone sleeps in while the rest of the family is awake, think of ways you can encourage the child to wake up earlier. For instance you could have a set bed-time and wakeup schedule or give responsibilities in the morning that will encourage everyone to wake up earlier. For each problematic situation come up with a potential solution.

In the rest of the book we're going to discuss common problems you may have with your child but in case you don't find the answers you are looking for, be prepared to do the research.

Before your new guest arrives make sure that you have already established household rules, that you would want **everyone** in your house to follow. The 'everyone' is highlighted because you don't want your foster child to feel like they are being singled out or treated unfairly compared to everyone else in the family. The household rules should also be rules that you yourself are willing to follow.

Some rules you may decide to have include; being respectful of other people and their property, picking up after yourself, telling the truth etc.

Deal With Your Own Reservations

This is not just your foster child's first day of school, it's yours too. Last minute jitters, cold feet or even outright fear are nothing to be ashamed of. They are more common than us foster parents are willing to admit because as adults, showing vulnerability isn't easy. You are receiving a stranger into your house. You don't know what to expect. Some of your friends and family may even warned you against it and put the fear of God into you (if I haven't already done that with my 'expect the worst' spiel). After all that, it would be odd if you were not a bit nervous. However you can't let this fear dissuade you from providing a home to that needy child.

How do you deal with the fear then? What works for me is to talk to someone who I trust and who is supportive of the work I am trying to do. It may be your partner or a trusted friend who will remind you of how much you are doing. Once in a while we all need a good ego boost. Another strategy is to think of yourself in the child's situation and imagine what it would feel like if you had no one to take you out of it. Empathy is a strong motivator.

You may not be the only one having problems either. If you have any other children and/or partner already living with you, they too may be experiencing the same nervous feelings. Have a family meeting to discuss the arrival of your new visitor. Talk about your family member's fears. Don't undermine these feelings. Instead discuss why you are doing this and what it will mean to the new child to finally have a nice home to stay. Reiterate that this is a new member of your family and as such they must treat them as such – fairly and respectfully.

Some members of your family may feel that the new addition is going to take your attention away from them. Reassure them that this is not the case. You are not abandoning them and that you always have time for them. If they are not familiar with your household rules, this is the time to introduce them. Emphasize that these will help you get along better as a family. You may also want to discuss what they should do if they have conflict with your new family member. Of course the first course of action is to tell you about it so that you can help them figure out a way to handle it.

You will find that this kind of advance mental preparation will help ease your fears and give you a sense of control.

Just Before That First Day

Apart from preparing yourself mentally for the challenges that will come with having a new guest, you will also need to prepare your environment for their entrance. The first thing you'll need to figure out is where your child will be sleeping. Most countries/states allow for children to share bedrooms if they are below a certain age or gender. However they do have to have a separate bed. I'm sure you've already sorted this out.

Get the beddings out for the child and set up the sleeping area. You will also need to set up a place for them to store their belongings.

Foster children are often very protective of their privacy and space so giving them somewhere exclusive is best. If you do not have a separate closet, a trunk would do. Try to make their space as inviting as possible. You may love the color white or dull colors but it only reminds the child of the clinical environment of homes they have been through. But also don't make it too bright that it seems like you're trying too hard. Colors like green, pale blue and purple would work really well for your foster child's space.

Have a quick check of the safety of your home. First things first keep all your medicine locked up and out of the reach of children. Make sure all your outlets are covered. I'm not saying you need prison bars, but you can reduce the probability of your child trying to run away by having grills on your windows, locks on your front and back doors so that at night you don't have to sleep with one eye open.

You will also need to have a list of things you want to ask the social worker when they bring the child home. Most will already have official information on school, parental visits and belongings but you need to know if the child has food allergies or strong dietary preferences, what kind of daily schedule they had in their previous home, performance in school, past behavioral problems, religious preferences and any medical needs that haven't been mentioned.

The social worker may not have all this information but you'll never know if you don't ask. Besides that the child will probably be a bit reluctant to share this information with you at first so any information you can get out of the social worker will be very helpful.

Once you do have this information, make appointments with all the other caregivers that you will be working with including the social worker him/herself, the child's teachers and doctors.

Finally to cap all your preparations get a welcome gift for your child. It doesn't have to be something expensive or big, just something personal. A gift tells the child that you are glad they are joining your family and it is something to be celebrated. It also shows that you care enough to think about them even before they got here. Gift ideas include a toy-car, a doll, a journal, a plastic watch – something that will leave them but is not so extravagant that they feel uncomfortable or like you're showing up their parents.

Immediately After Entry

Unless you are getting a baby, your foster child will probably come to you in a state of sadness, heart-broken, grieving or wanting to go back home so your first task is to make them feel wanted. Let him/her know that you are excited to have them here and that they are welcome into your home. The gift will act as a physical symbol of how happy for their presence in their home.

If they are able to talk ask them what they would like you to call them. I know that the social worker has probably provided you with their legal names but children, just like you, have their preferences of which names or nicknames they prefer. Little things like these help them become more comfortable in their new home and show them that you are respectful of who they are.

For most new foster parents the question is what they should call you. There are arguments for and against them calling you mommy and/or daddy. The cons include the probability of forming too much of an attachment that they won't be able to let you go. The pros include that it makes the child feel more a part of a family. My opinion is that it depends on the child.

For some children have been shifted between so many homes that mommy and daddy has become a function and not a person (they call you 'the mommy' or 'the daddy'). Introduce yourself by your first name because surnames are way too authoritarian and will only add formality you don't need. If the child chooses to call you mommy or daddy because it makes them feel a part of the family, don't make a big deal of it, just roll with it.

Introduce your foster to the other children as their new friend. Some parents introduce the foster child as new brother or sister. I advice against this as it sets up expectations in both your children and your foster child that this arrangement is permanent. In all probability it isn't. In later chapters we'll talk about how to let your child know that you are not their 'forever' family but for now, your task is to make sure that they are comfortable in their new home.

Don't immediately launch into a run-down of your family's dos and don'ts. Give the child a day or two day reprieve to get used to their new home. During this reprieve you can have further activities to let them get used to living in your home. This you can do by going about your day as you normally would and according to your schedule. This way they will get a sense of your family schedule and behavior without the pressure to conform.

Look for ways to enhance their comfort such as asking them what their favorite foods are and looking for ways to incorporate them into your weekly menu. Ask them if they like their room. Even little things like allowing them to change the position of the bed or pick a color for their duvet will make them more at ease. If you have a child who won't talk some reconnaissance (covert observation) may be needed.

After the reprieve you can finally have private sit-down with them. This private sit down should be just between the primary care-giver and the child. The whole family is a definite no-no and two adults may be intimidating enough to cause the child to shut down. In this sit-down you'll need to talk about how they feel so far about their new home. What they would like from you and your family? If it is something you can do, express it. If not explain why.

Express what you expect from them in terms of schedule and behavior and introduce them to your household rules. Ask them if they understand the household rules and if there is anything they would like to add to them. This one-on-one should be as light as possible. You are not lecturing them, just talking. Show them that you respect their opinions and trust their ability to meet all your expectations.

Chapter 2:
Providing The Normalcy Of Family Life

Some children take a day to adjust to living with your family, some take a week, some a month…others never will. That is the nature of fostering. However most parents start off very eager to transition the child into normalcy. They end up pushing and pushing for the child to immediately fit in. Meanwhile, the child, who isn't ready to be transitioned, pulls further away from the caregiver or resents him/her because they feel they are being rushed.

Remember that your child already has their own version of normalcy. It will take a while for them to get used to your version of normal. So take it at their pace. Step by step.

Have The Family Schedule Up

You may have memorized your schedule, but your foster child certainly hasn't. Have a written version of what every member of the family should be doing at each hour of the day somewhere. For younger children, make the schedule as pretty as possible using different materials and colors. For both older and younger children, make it as interactive as possible. Get them to help you write it out and stick it up. You would be surprised at how much being involved in the creation of the schedule will encourage them to follow it.

Because they are new to the schedule, providing some kind of motivation like a reward to keep to the schedule at first may be necessary. It doesn't have to be a extravagant or even physical. Such rewards like an extra hour of sleeping or TV during the weekend, a book they wanted, a creamy desert on a day that you usually wouldn't, or their favorite food could go a long way in encouraging them.

Have a calendar of important events for both them and the rest of your family up on the fridge or cupboard that they are allowed to add to.

Give Responsibilities

In Chapter One you've introduced your child to your family's dos and don'ts, it's now time to make them an actual part of the family by giving them responsibilities just like you do with the rest of your family. Responsibility is not just a way for you to feel less burdened. It makes them feel included and is a growth process for your foster children. It teaches them that being part of a family and the society means contributing to its well being.

Give your foster child a way to contribute to your family through chores, whether it is washing the dishes at the end of the day, helping you with clean up on weekends, making their beds in the morning etc. Even little ones can be given small tasks like picking up their toys at the end of day and placing them in the correct place. Give them something to do that is appropriate to their age and is fair when compared to what the rest of your family members are doing. Of course some children may feel like they shouldn't have to do anything but explain that families help one another and that they are now part of your family.

To ease their transition into your 'normal' introduce these responsibilities one by one. Once they have mastered one, you can add another. If they are not familiar with how you do things, be appreciative of what contribution they have made. For instance if the child washes the dishes but they are not as clean as you would like them, praise them for the effort. Later you can show them how you like it done.

They probably also have pre-existing ideas of how things are done. Don't shut those down, ask them to show you. If they are better than yours, you can incorporate them into your own way of living, if not then explain why. This shows how appreciative you are of them and the contribution they are making.

Champion Learning and School

School is an important part of any child's life, your foster child included. We all know the benefits of education. It helps ease your transition into working life much faster and raises your standards of living.

For a foster child school is even more important because unlike 'normal' children they often do not have a support system like parent/relatives who will help them out in case they do not do so well in their future life. Education will allow them create their own source and income after they are out of the system. Despite this critical role that education will play in their life and because of the upheavals in their life, foster children tend to under-perform.

Because different types of upheaval cause a different kind of reaction to school in your child, we will take sample scenarios and discuss ways in which you can deal them.

Child One has been shifted between different homes and different locations so often that is has left a large gap in their learning. The change in classrooms means other students are either ahead of them or behind them. Your solution for this is to have the whole syllabus for their stage of education at your disposal. The teacher will probably have this or you can also access it through the internet. Start by giving the child practice-exercises for each of the topics in the syllabus to see what their mastery of them is. If they have problems with any of the topics, talk to their teacher about extra classes, help out as much as you can or hire a tutor for them.

Like Child One, Child Two has been moved regularly. They however come with an extra problem; the constant shift has left them discouraged to put effort into learning because they know that any day now they will have to move into another home and/or another school. I knew a child who had been moved through eleven different foster/group/shelter homes – and she was only fifteen.

For such children, don't give them false expectations that they won't be moved because you have no control over that. Focus instead on helping them with the coping skills for this constant shift. Make sure they have their syllabus at their disposal so that they feel more control over their own learning. Also enlist the help of their therapist because this is an emotional issue and you may need some backup.

Child Three under-performs because it is hard for them to get back into the daily routine of life, of which school is part of, after the upheaval they have gone through. It is hard for them to focus and complete class-work and homework. More than any other child, this foster child needs to have a schedule that will help them regain their sense of focus.

Have a regular time for homework when all the members of your family sit down and complete their assignments for the day. Sit down with them or make yourself available for any help they may need. Check their books at the end of the day to make sure they not only attended class but also participated in it by doing all the expected work. Keep in constant contact with the teacher so that you know how they are doing. At first they may resist it but with time and your own constancy, you can transition them into it.

Child Four under-performs but does not know the reason why so s/he attributes it to their being dumber than other children. Usually a child like this will be isolated or aggressive in school because they feel inadequate when compared with other children. Once you have discovered that this is the problem, you need to reassure him/her that they are just as good as the other children, only they've had a harder time in school. Explain that it is possible to catch up.

With such a child comparing them to other children

is especially counter-productive. Instead their yard stick should be themselves. If the child got an E in the last test and brings home a D- this week, don't be worried that so and so had a B or an A.

Your concern should be that they improved. Celebrate the child's improvement then set new targets for them. Step by step you can get them to where their peers are.

Child Five hates school because of all the above factors and more. A common behavior for this type of child is that either they shut down during class or just skip. Before this child can even get into the learning mindset they need to understand why learning is important to them. I'm not talking about dousing your child with all the doomsday predictions like one out of four children who ages out of foster care will be homeless by the end of the year because of no means of income. Focus on showing your child the benefits of a good education.

Practical demonstrations are more important than words in this case. When making your week's budget, show them you wouldn't be able to calculate the cost of things if you didn't have Math skills or you job to give you that money to spend.

Ask them who are their role-models and show them how education has benefited these people or how it could it add to their satisfaction with their jobs. Take 'bring your child to work' days as an opportunity to show them how much working is important.

Talking to your child may help you figure out what scenario you are dealing with. If you still have no idea then remember the best thing to do is get involved in your child's learning by checking assignments and following what they are learning in school. Encourage them to perform better by explaining the benefits of education, setting a routine, setting performance targets and providing extra learning help as needed. Maintain constant contact with their teacher. The teachers are a great resource to help you learn more about your child's learning and to get ahead of any issues before they get out of hand.

Make the experience as positive as possible for both of you. Make learning fun by reading bed-time stories to them, playing games that subtly encourage learning, use books as a reward for achievements. If there are any fun extra-curricular activities that the child is supposed to take part in in school such as field trips, sports etc, show your support by providing the resources as well as the moral support needed by the child.

Don't let your child feel out of place when the rest of their classmates are doing something. If everyone is required to bring a story book for library time, make sure to pack them one. Sometimes they may not tell you because they feel like they are being a burden to you. This is where it is even more important to maintain constant communication with your child's teachers so that you know what is going on in school even before they tell you.

Most important of all, realize that this is a process. You're not going to wake up tomorrow and have an A student. In fact you may never have an A student. However, just the act of caring enough about their future to help them out with their schooling will have more of an impact on your child then you'll probably ever know. Someone cares.

Handle Their Day-to-Day Needs

Part of being a good parent is making sure that your child's needs are met including their leisure, dietary and medical needs. You need to make sure your foster child receives the hours of sleep that are necessary for a child of their age each and every night. They may come to you unused to having a bedtime schedule and getting them on yours may be a hard task.

Have a set bedtime and bedtime routines that clue them in that it is time to shut down for the day. Such routines include putting off the TV at a certain time each night, having them shower and then brush their teeth before settling into their beds. Make sure that their sleeping environment is comfortable enough i.e. not too hot or cold so that it doesn't interfere with their sleep patterns.

On average it takes a child three to fourteen days to get used to a new sleep schedule so the first days may need your patience and commitment. Do not use early sleep as a punishment because your foster child will associate sleeping with negative emotions and therefore be more resistant to your efforts.

When it comes to food, your child may have preconceived notions of what they eat but you can retrain them too or at least encourage them to eat better. The first step to that is to know what their previous diet was like before they came to your house. Ask them what their favorite foods are and include them into at least one meal in your weekly plan (even if it is junk food).

If you want to introduce them to better eating habits such as taking in more veggies and fruits, involve them in the process of their creation. When you are doing your weekly shopping, take them to the grocery with you and allow them to choose some of the vegetables you will be eating and invite them to help you cook. It will make them more likely to eat when it finally lands on the table. Remember that the point of the exercise is to get them to eat healthier so any choice they make is a good choice.

If there is a food that you feel may be unfamiliar to them, just serve it. Say nothing at all about the unfamiliar food (including how you think they don't know what it is) during mealtime. Just let them find their way around it. If they don't eat it at all, *then* you can talk about it. Encourage them to have even just a small portion of the food so that it doesn't feel that overwhelming to them. As the days go by you can increase their portion size of the new food.

As concerns their medical needs make sure you have

is a First Aid box that is fully functional. Consider getting some basic First Aid training so that you know how to respond during emergency situations. All foster children are usually eligible for your government's medical aid but it is important to find out exactly what services are available under it.

You also need to know who the closest covered 24 hour medical-care provider to your home is. You never know when your child will get sick in the middle of the night and you need to get them to a doctor. If your child has any special medical needs, make sure to ask your social worker about how you should cater for these, any specialists they need to see and the financial ramifications (if any) to you.

Most children are required to visit a therapist. Not everyone accepts the value of therapy and your child may come with a preconceived notion of what it is, making them reluctant to attend these sessions. You need to make sure that despite this, your child makes their appointment each and every time. Not only is therapy good for your child as it helps them deal with their issues, it is also good for you. You will have less behavioral issues to deal with.

If possible you should schedule a meeting of your own with the therapist to discuss ways in which you can ease your child's adjustment to their new home.

Deal with Weekends, Holidays and Vacations

I've put weekends, holidays and vacations as a separate function from your daily schedule because more often than not, this is when unexpected activities that you and/or your foster child do not expect happen.

The first thing to remember is to inform the child well in advance whenever a special activity is supposed to occur. For instance, if you have a trip to the park on Saturday, don't just spring it on them on Saturday morning. Coming from homes where order isn't all that common, the last thing they need is laissez-faire parenting. Even one day notice will do.

Include them in everything that the rest of your family members will be doing be it extended family get togethers, neighbourhood potlucks, marathons you are running... They may decline – but invite them each and every time. The very act of inviting them shows that you care of them.

Now you're probably wondering what to do when they decline. Encourage but don't force the issue. Part of successful transitioning is to let the child make the decision to become an active part of your family. However, if not forcing the issue means that they have to stay at home, find a caregiver to look after them. Reiterate that you would prefer that they go with you because you will miss them and their company but that it is their choice.

Before you give up on them however, you need to find out why they don't want to come with you. Listen empathetically to their reason and find alternative solutions that mean they don't stay with away from your family.

You may find that the problem isn't that they want to stay at home but rather that they are afraid of having to interact with strange people. Some solutions for such a situation would be to tell them what to expect from the event, who will be there, suggest that you stay with them till they are comfortable enough to mingle and/or enlist your family's help in 'taking care' of your foster child during the event.

Holidays are especially hard for foster children. Already your child is feeling abandoned, lost and/or lonely (yes it is possible to be lonely even if you are not alone) and are struggling with the desire to see their relatives even when they haven't been that good to them. Holidays just make these feelings more acute because tradition demands that this is when you should be with your family. Add on the guilt that comes from enjoying themselves when they know that in all likelihood their relatives are not having as good a time as they are having and there is every probability that you will have a dour child on your hands during the holidays.

It's hard to enjoy yourself when a member of your

family is obviously not having a good time. Other members of your family will pick up on your child's dampened mood and react in different ways. It is perfectly normal for some to be resentful because their new friend is 'spoiling' Christmas or New Year or Hanukah.

In such situations, it is up to you as the parents to make sure the holidays don't end up too awkward. For the sake of your own family maintain the cheery mood all around and do not cancel any of your family traditions. For your foster child don't confront them about how badly they are behaving. Instead encourage them to get involved by asking them to help with hanging up holiday decorations, cooking and giving them gifts.

Later, maybe during bedtime, have a one-one talk with them expressing that you understand their feelings. Encourage them to share with you stories about their favorite holidays with their 'forever' family and what they did. If they want, incorporate some of their holiday traditions into your own. If you are a praying family, pray with them for the well-being of their family so that they are aware that you care not just for them but for where they are from.

If all this is still not working for you, it's time to call for rescue. Some extra sessions with their therapist may help your foster child deal with his/her abandonment issues.

In the case of go-away vacations, always remember

that you need to check with the social worker first before you take the child out of the city/state. If you're not allowed to take them out but this was something you had planned with your family, discuss what options are available for the child while you're away. Remember that you also have your own family and they should not have to feel like they are losing out because of your new addition.

Dealing with Visitations

Since the goal of foster care is reunification, there will probably be supervised visits between the child and their parents or other relatives. If you have advance notice of the visit, inform the child in advance by telling them when the visit will occur and why.

Show excitement about the visit even if you do not feel it because the child will take their cues from you. Encourage them to wear their best clothes because this is a special day for both them and their parent/relative.

In most cases, you won't be expected to attend the visitation. However there are times you may come in contact with the child's parents or relatives in waiting rooms or such. Many foster parents will tell you that dealing with the child's parents or relatives can often be almost as hard as dealing with the child him/herself. There are the amazing cases where the relatives are just glad that there was someone to pick the ball when they weren't able. Then there are cases where the relatives transfer their feelings of inadequacy and/or being unfairly treated by the state to you because you are now the physical representation of an unjust system. I have experienced this kind of hostility more times than I can count.

The best thing to do is to first take it away from the child's area of vision or hearing. You don't want the child to see the most important people in their family fighting. They've already had enough of that. If you get a chance to talk to the parent/relative, emphasize that you are not trying to take their child away from them. You are teammates not competitors. Your role is to hold the forte down for them till the state (not you) feels that they are ready to take back their child. You have no control over it.

If you're feeling especially frustrated, put yourself in the parents' shoes. Imagine a situation where your own child was taken away from you to be brought up by strangers how would you feel? I bet you would have some issues too. Avoid making judgment calls on their fitness as parents because you do not know the story behind the story and it is not your role anyway.

Chapter 3:
Dealing With Behavioral Issues

There is a lot of baggage that comes with someone from the kind of background your child has. Some of this baggage may include a lack of self control, aggression towards people, animals and/or property, disrespect to authority, little self help and hygiene skills.

Behavioral issues are not something you can handle in a day, not even a week. It will take you time and sometimes help. Let's discuss a few ways that you can deal with this baggage before and when it starts to show.

Set Yourself Up For Success

Even before the issues occur you need to know when to reward and when to punish and when to do nothing. How do you decide what's punishable and what's reward-worthy? Consider where they are coming from and what their normal there was. If they never ever ate vegetables in their previous environment then you can reward them till it becomes their new habit.

When their grace period is over and they have learnt the new habit and you can stop the rewards. If it is a behavior that is completely unacceptable then a punishment should be attached to it. For instance don't reward the child for not hitting others but punish them if they do.

Once you know what will be rewarded, punished and is just normal (so no punishment or not), decide on the rewards and punishments. If better grades mean a trip to the theatre to watch their favorite movie instead of borrowing it in your local video store, the child will be more likely to put more effort into homework and studying for tests.

If the children know that for every extra hour of TV they watch, they are risking an hour of their turn on the internet or with their friends, they are less likely to watch that hour. If throwing a tantrum will land them in the naughty corner for six minutes, then tell them in advance so that when they throw a tantrum they know exactly what to expect.

The consequence should match the offence. Firm, fair and clear boundaries teach the child controls. Many times you will need to explain each rule for the child and why it is in place so be ready with reasons that the child will understand. Make sure the rules apply to everyone. More than any other child, children dealing with abandonment issues feel unfairness. If the child feels that they are not being singled out, they will be more likely to follow your set rules.

Unintentional Mistakes

Despite your best efforts, sometimes the child may forget the rules you have already set. It's not deliberate, it just happens.

Despite how empathetic you may feel, do not let it slide 'just this one time' because it will continue to happen again and 'I forgot' will be your child's trademark excuse. Instead, take the time out to explain what the mistake is, the agreement you and the child had and that you have to keep to the agreement.

If the offence has to do with habits they have acquired before, don't expect perfection immediately. For such offences, don't set hard rules, instead set performance targets that you will reward. Once the new habit has become their 'normal' then you can set it as a hard rule.

For instance if the child doesn't use the toilet but instead urinates all around the house, your first target would be just to get them to go to the bathroom. Once they have achieved that then your next target would be to get them to the toilet. If the child is used to dealing with confrontation by turning it into a physical altercation, just getting them to stop hitting and yell the problem is a first step.

Gradually you can help them learn how to redirect their anger by expressing their frustration in a calm tone or walking away from it.

Deliberate Flaunting of Rules

Sometimes their breaking of rules may be deliberate. This is especially common with older children who are either testing or rebelling against authority.

Enforcing rules consistently helps with a child who is testing you. They want to see if the consequence today will be the same as the consequence tomorrow. They are basically just looking for a constant in their life and are looking to you as the adult to provide it (albeit in the wrong way). So do what you say you'll do – each and every time.

The child who is rebelling against authority is a bit more difficult to deal with because often they are taking out their hurt on you and normal disciplinary measures work very slowly. In this situation, it is even more important for you to maintain your own self-control. Frustration is a normal reaction but you need to control your own anger and not show it overtly, after all this is what you are trying to teach your child. Do not get into a yelling match with them. It is the absolute worst thing you can do. Instead give yourself and the child time to cool down before you talk about the issue again and the consequences later.

During this time-out find an outlet for your anger. Your outlet may include calming exercises and talking to someone about the problem. Someone else may be able to see the problem objectively and give you valuable insight into how to deal with the issue. When you do come back you will feel more in control of the situation. And come back you must – don't let matters lie just because dealing with them is uncomfortable for you.

If the child has an anger problem, you may need to help them find an outlet of their own. Ask them what their favorite thing to do for instance drawing, singing, reading and running. Sure your child may like to sing at the top of her voice when they are angry. It may be irritating but it sure is better than the black eyes she keeps giving other children. Encourage them to do this hobby when they are angry. Gradually their outlet may help them develop more positive feeling.

Do not compare their behavior to that of other children. Using siblings as an example of good behavior will only make the 'good' sibling the subject of disdain and jealousy while the 'bad' sibling becomes the target of judgment. Consider the child as his own being – meaning compare their past to their present.

If two months ago Cindy would often steal food from the refrigerator and hide it in their room be appreciative that these days she asks if she can eat in her room (even though what you really want is for her to eat with the rest of their family).

If it is a behavior that is embarrassing, celebrate with them privately one on one. This is the way they know that you appreciate their improvement without getting embarrassed in front of the whole family.

When To Involve A Third Party

Sometimes regardless of what you do, it may not be enough. There are just some children who require more help then you are capable of giving. When your efforts are having no visible effects and the behavior is having an effect on theirs or your family's safety, it is time to call in the cavalry. Talk to one of your team members, be it their social worker and/or therapist, and explain the exact nature of the problem so that they can intervene.

Never be afraid to ask for help. As long as you have done your best, you are not failing the child. As we have said before, your child came into your home with years of abuse, emotional upheaval, mistreatment along with other baggage, some of which you don't even know about.

The fact that you are asking for help rather than wallowing away in frustration means that you want the best for them and know when you are not the most qualified person to deal with it.

Chapter 4:
Taking Care Of Yourself

Now that you know what the experience of fostering your child is like, I'm sure you understand why it is so important for you to take care of yourself. As rewarding an experience as fostering is, it comes with its own challenges and to deal with them you will need to keep up your own physical and emotional health.

Being healthy isn't just for you. As the care-giver for children, still developing, you are the role-model for the kind of adult they should grow into. They have seen enough adults in crisis. They do not need to see you go down the same path.

Your Physical Health

Keeping your body in good condition should be one of your daily goals. When you are physically healthy it doesn't just increase your life-span but it allows you to serve your family as best as you can.

There are five main components of maintaining your body eating healthy, exercising each day, resting well and seeking medical attention when you need it.

Your body needs not just fuel but the proper kind of fuel to run. Eat a balanced diet that contains the proper kinds of nutrients each day in the proper proportions. I know that you are probably already running around the house trying to take care of everyone but take at least thirty minutes of exercise like taking a walk or some yoga. Exercise is not just good for your body it's good for your mind too. Those thirty minutes help you release endorphins that reduce strengths.

No matter how busy your day is, get at least six to eight hours of sleep each night. Sleep gives your body time to recover from all the miles you are putting it through during the day. Quality rest makes you a better care-giver because you are not fatigued. Children, fostered or biological, deserve a well rested mother.

As caregivers we often neglect our own medical needs to take care of our families. You are not doing anyone any favors. Apart from the probability that you could be contagious, your bad health reduces your capacity to take care of them. The sooner you seek medical attention, the sooner you can get back to parenting form.

Your Emotional Health

Not only do you need to maintain your body's condition, you also need to make sure that you are emotionally healthy. Taking care of foster kids takes a lot of dedication, sacrifice and strength and everyday you need to bolster your emotional health. The first way to do this is to create and maintain 'grown-up' relationships.

As much as you are tempted to give all your time to your children, your grown-up relationships serve as a support system for you. Foster children are in great emotional need and this can be draining to you. Where do you go when you need that boost to keep on keeping on?

Don't neglect your relationships. If you have a partner, take some time out to build and maintain your relationship. You should have time each day that is just between the two of you where you can talk about everything and nothing as well as reiterate your support for each other. Every once in a while you should take some time away from the family. Most states/countries allow you to hire a babysitter is over eighteen years old to look after your foster child(ren) for the night while you and your partner get to know each other again.

If you do not have a partner, you should at the very least have a confidant who you can talk to about your daily challenges as well as triumphs on the regular. There are also many support groups out there for foster parents where you can discuss your troubles, learn from other more experienced parents and even share your own tips.

If you cannot find a physical group that is close to you, consider joining an online group or participating in active online blogs such as http://foster-care.adoptionblogs.com where you can meet other foster parents. These blogs can also help connect you to other training opportunities that will help you become a much better foster parent.

If you feel overwhelmed to the point that your support system isn't helping, consider seeing a therapist. A completely objective eye can help you discover issues you didn't even know were plaguing you and teach you healthy ways to deal with the stress you might experience as a result of being a foster parent.

Take care of yourself and you'll be better at taking care of others.

Chapter 5:
Letting Go

The aim of foster care is to reunify the child with their biological family. You need to remind yourself this every time you take on a new child. More often than not you will develop maternal or paternal feelings for these children and start to think of them as your own.

That, unfortunately, is the bane of being a foster parent. It's not like you can decide to withhold your affections back to protect yourself when it is finally time for the child to walk away. The only thing you can do is to ease the child's exit out of your life both for you and the child.

Before you even know if they will be leaving, the child should be aware that this is not their 'forever' home.

More often than not the child will bring up the topic all on their own.

You'll receive questions like why can't you be their child, or when will their own parents be coming for them. There are honestly no magic words you can say that will make the conversation easier. The best you can do is to be honest about their situation but do not be brutal about it.

Do not lie to the child, do not set their expectations too high and do not skirt around the issue to save their feeling. Believe me, they know when you do. If adoption is something you are considering, never mention it till you are sure that it will be happening.

Your social worker will more often than not give you advance notice of when the child is supposed to leave your house. Inform the child of when they will be leaving. Discuss their feelings and reservations with them and reassure them that the new people they are going to live with will provide just as good a home as you have.

Once the child is informed you can inform the rest of your family about their departure. It may cause some distress but a family meeting can help deal with this. In some cases you may be allowed to keep some sort of communication with your foster child (ask the social worker first). If it is an option explain to your family that they will steal have an opportunity to talk to each other.

If possible organize for a small going away party for your little one where you can invite their closest new friends and your family members. The party is as much for you as it is for them because it helps you come to terms with their exit. Give them a gift that they can use to remember you with and if they want they can give you something they'd like you to remember them from. Take lots and lots of pictures during your small party.

Most of the time when the child is about to leave, they will be eased into it either by starting off with weekly visits, then overnights which will eventually lead to permanent stay. At each stage, inform the child of the changes that will be taking place and why it is taking place. On the final day of exit, you can even take the day off to say good-bye to them.

If the exit is abrupt (you did not have any kind of notice) do what you can to make it special. They came to your house abruptly. You don't want them leaving the same way. Many foster parents have a stash of gifts that they keep on the ready. The important thing is to let the child know that they will be missed and remembered.

After the child has left, take the time to grieve. This is a person that you had grown attached to who has left your life. Your family members had also gotten used to their new friend and are now at a loss at their exit.

Grieving is an important component of letting go.

Have a family meeting where you can talk about the child and have some sort of ritual that you can use to help each other. Some families write a letter to the child telling them how much they miss them and wishing them well with their new family.

Even if you are not allowed to communicate after the exit, just the act of writing the letter and expressing your feelings helps you get a better handle on the loss. Use the photos you have to create scrap books or collages that you can pin on your wall. If your family is a praying family include the child and their new family in their prayers. If you get any news about the child, share it with your family so that they are reassured that their family member is okay. With time the ache will recede but you do have to give it time.

Conclusion

hank you again for buying this book!

I hope this book was able to help you to deal with the joys and challenges that come with being a foster parent. The work you are doing now is noble work. There are more children than you know out there who need a family today. I may not have provided all the answers but I hope you have gained some insight into being a better foster parent.

Finally, if you enjoyed this book, please take the time to share your thoughts and post a review on Amazon. It'd be greatly appreciated!

Thank you and good luck!

ALL RIGHTS RESERVED. No part of this publication may be reproduced or transmitted in any form whatsoever, electronic, or mechanical, including photocopying, recording, or by any informational storage or retrieval system without express written, dated and signed permission from the author.

DISCLAIMER AND/OR LEGAL NOTICES: Every effort has been made to accurately represent this book and it's potential. Results vary with every individual, and your results may or may not be different from those depicted. No promises, guarantees or warranties, whether stated or implied, have been made that you will produce any specific result from this book. Your efforts are individual and unique, and may vary from those shown. Your success depends on your efforts, background and motivation.

The material in this publication is provided for educational and informational purposes only and is not intended as medical advice. The information contained in this book should not be used to diagnose or treat any illness, metabolic disorder, disease or health problem. Always consult your physician or health care provider before beginning any nutrition or exercise program. Use of the programs, advice, and information contained in this book is at the sole choice and risk of the reader. Neither the author nor the publisher shall be liable for any emotional, psychological, physical, commercial or financial damages, nor for to any other damages. References are provided for informational purposes only and do not constitute endorsement of any websites or other sources. Readers should be aware that the websites listed in this book may change

Made in the USA
Lexington, KY
24 June 2016